Heart
a folk-h...

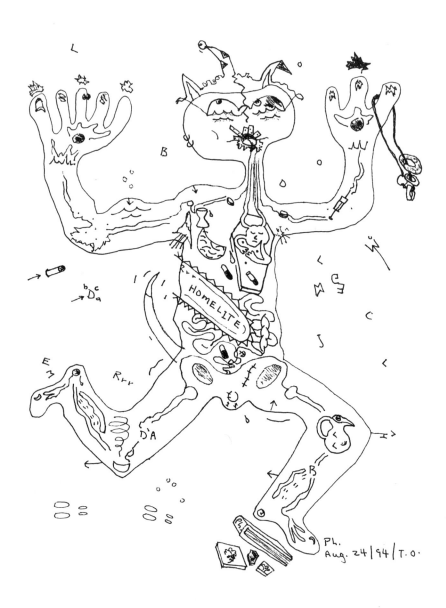

HoMELiTE

Ph.
Aug. 24/94/T.O.

HEARTHEDRAL
A FOLK-HERMETIC

Phil Hall

Ph.
April 23/05

Brick Books

CANADIAN CATALOGUING IN PUBLICATION DATA

Hall, Phil
 Hearthedral : a folk-hermetic

Poems.
ISBN 0-919626-87-4

I. Title.

PS8565.A449H43 1996   C811'.54   C96-931324-1
PR9199.3.H35H43 1996

The support of the Canada Council and the Ontario Arts Council
is gratefully acknowledged. The support of the Government of
Ontario through the Ministry of Culture, Tourism and Recreation
is also gratefully acknowledged.

The cover photograph is of the rear window of Christ Anglican
Church, Bobcaygeon, Ontario (Goddard & Gibbs, 1952),
Peterborough Tourist Board.

The back cover photograph is of a window in the Toronto Dance
Theatre, and is by Marianne McLeod. The inside cover sketch is
by Linda Gustafson. The title page etching is by D'Arcy Hall.
Other drawings are by the author.

Typeset in Ehrhardt, printed and bound by The Porcupine's
Quill. The stock is acid-free Zephyr Antique laid.

Brick Books
431 Boler Road, Box 20081
London, Ontario
N6K 4G6

Schwermut-Granit wird mein Blut
(Meloncholy-Granite become my Blood)
Nelly Sachs

An animal's an outburst, with a steeple
Heather McHugh

this one's for Brett (*psommi*)

Townes Van Zandt
('the dust that Poncho bit down south
ended up in Lefty's mouth' – *botrys*)

& 'the Stubborns'
(who are – as Osip Mandelstam explains –
'a race much older than the Romans')

I too have written the little square ones
now let us admit unto this assemblage an *ours etc.*

w/ D'Arcy, Dale & Glen, Chris & Catherine, D. Jane, Stan

w/ readers: Andrew Vaisius, Erin Mouré, Robert Pepper-Smith

w/ the Ontario Arts Council, *West Coast Line*, *What!*,
Books in Canada

w/ Audrey Karlinski, James Deutsch, Schlomo Goldhaber

w/ my former colleagues at *This Magazine*, my fellow residents
at Three Streets Housing Co-op …

& the inconspicuous erudition
of my editor, Marnie Parsons

Introductory

Iroquois, *etc.* & **Steam,** *etc.*: these lists are borrowed from 'Spadina Line,' a public-art installation by Brad Golden and Norman Richards. Comprised of 'switch-post' lights & metal words, this work runs along Spadina Avenue north of Dupont Road in Toronto. (We must, of course, credit Golden & Richards with the intrinsic poetry that exists in the lists themselves.)

An official lamp lighting ceremony for the installation took place on September 21, 1991.

These lists suggest developments from wild to rural to urban Ontario land; they also echo the small, long-gone railways that used to service mining towns & villages to the north.

In this poem these lists accrue parallel, private words & meanings from wild to rural to urban, and in so doing become word-girders for a cathedral of low sorts.

A funeral is underway: the will has died. Pipes play the pibroch.

As David Jones says in his introduction to *The Anathemata*: 'to make a shape out of the very things of which one is oneself made.'

Canada is also dead. When nationhood is lost without resistance, hermetic & idiosyncratic chapels of selfhood may still be worthy of defence and maintenance – toward (however covert and puny) some other uncompromiseable community.

Built of hearth units between list pages, and culminating in central spires of longtall parts, this poem aspires to a structure – a possible section scheme of which is:

```
                          ^
            7           7
            6           6
          5 5         5 5
        4 4 4       4 4 4
        3 3 3       3 3 3 3
      2 2 2 2       2 2 2 2 2
  0 0 1 1 1 1       1 1 1 1 1 0 0
```

Thanks to the City of Toronto Archives,

Phil Hall, Cabbagetown, 1992-1996

from willseed sprout
hearthedral

(Huckleberry gargoyle
Blind Pew vaulted archway

Micawbered buttress)
above ladders chamois

circling inlaid domes
ungonged firebells

empty pews
blank hymnals

this mortarsinew chorus
will succeed

You will know when the poem begins
but reading shan't accomplish this alone

go to St. Clair W. & Spadina in Toronto
walk south on Spadina over the ravine bridge
& uphill to Casa Loma

where the road curves east of the gates
go along the park path of the east wall

if the fountain is on at the head of the stairs
take a sip in honour of the lake once up to here
(none of this may still exist)

(a piper is roostering from a chapel downwind
urlar, siabhal, taorluath, crunluath*)*

then descend to Davenport Rd.
cross at the lights & begin to read
words at intervals in the sidewalk

each word under a little streetlight
of its own (Iroquois, Furrow ...)

after Archive
pass under Dupont Railway Bridge
(sniff memory of creosote)

& there on the west wall
of the underpass read train words
(Steam, Whistle ...)

these are the stations
of Ontario's ruralness aspiring
(you will know when the poem begins)
(none of this may still exist)

do this fieldwork
as if pacing page jurisdiction
as if a walk could be a read

singed thong   **Iroquois**   *inflank*
                          Furrow
                          Survey
                          Avenue
                          Power
                          Dairy
                          Archive

Glacial Lake

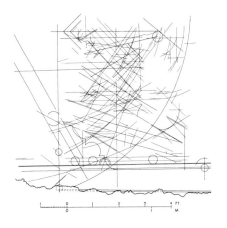

as the feast begins
the son is on the floor
in the foetal position

under his knees & over his elbows
a broomstick has been shoved
& his hands tied at his shins

the rounded point of the stick against linoleum
props him from falling completely onto his side

the broom's old bristles poise above him
a hand the floor has molted to a scythe

his family's eyes shut
to the listing gravy boat

then turkey is fine tooth combed
for its emergency flight record
of the year's last moments

the Pope's nose haggled over
& the wishbone hung behind the stove pipe

Official Guardian
pull the broom through the little captain
our only hope

'you will recall my baby toes
have no nails
            mere indentations
from which poke soft claws

today off from the **chonk & halloo**
of sample gathering

I faced multifoliate depth's insurgence

the sea's ranging lip undercupping & baling

sand first ebony
stretched to mushroom purple

then foxed parchment
pulled from bankrupt purple

foxed parchment
drawn & quartered to loam

as outward from my provincial digits
cemetery ambition fanned its palette

a yet unencountered creature's soul
shivered through me
                        & glanced unflinchingly
at my filigree from inside!

a coal smoke & cream chivas
stingray moth of sand seemed to leak
or be sucked from me!

cease praying for my return   . . .

my exhausted finery
shall strut in a masque
of gnashed tendons

my baby toes
(that were dwarfs at court)

here shall be ancestral hinges
the eyes of inedible yams'

a witness nerve in the brain crimps
& months each word a stripped th/read

nosepierced momace pawfete typuns on
hollow bean wards stuffed w/ elephones

then one day the next pinched moment is
unpinched
        a settlement after hummocks

and I can talk
of Schlomo Goldhaber on burial duty

in the camp a couple frozen
seated facing each other holding hands

by wrongs they should have been separated
with a shovel and flattened and thrown on

but Schlomo and his detail
dug a grave deep and let them go in
alone still seated holding

to tell some stories is to stand
in ice skates on a garden hose

a witness nerve in the brain crimps
visionwary

hearth gods
coddle potential

service machines
domestic

bonding spirits putter
cornerstone senses

(incessantly ink &
erase **I / It**)

sacrosanctities
replenish molespirit's

impalpable
sustenance

cutworm

Iroquois
Furrow
Survey
Avenue
Power
Dairy
Archive

creamfork

gravy

Steam
Whistle
Schedule
Chestnut
Coal

swangel

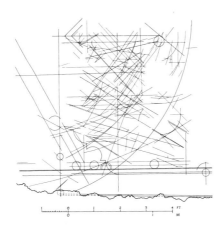

this is not me
this is a photograph of me

sigmature of a man who pretends to be me
farce with me in the role of me

this man dreams of me
dreams he is me

apes me
does a spitting image of me

this is a self portrait of me by not me
reflected askew

this man believes he is me
everyone believes him to be me

but I myself do not fall for it
this is me

attention is the natural prayer of the soul
                    Malebranche

negligence and irregularity, long continued, will make knowledge
useless, wit ridiculous, and genius contemptible
                    Johnson (on Savage)

— *I Should Fall From Grace With God*
                    The Pogues

doubtaffirming quotes
come to tune out walls

of this bachelor
hearth body station

in which planed oak radio waves
blare unscotched untaped

& 5 coupled elongated O's
of radiator have silverash

but handsewn Tree Of Life shirt
soft maple leaves off balcony

taskmasts unfurled calm
outwaiting Need St. & Snake Pt. Rd.

a chance at love
tenacious ease

daughtersnore on futon
son coming to make me sing

'Pretty Boy Floyd' again & rub his back
this mortarsinew chorus
                    succeed

What if one changed the needle and directed it on its return journey along a tracing which was not derived from the graphic translation of a sound, but existed of itself naturally – well: to put it plainly, along the coronal suture, for example. What would happen? A sound would necessarily result, a series of sounds, music … what variety of lines then, occurring anywhere, could one not put under the needle and try out?

Rilke (G. Craig Houston)

where pulp gives way to skin
as skin & air abut (magnified whizz)
Levi blows pipe smoke into Dot's ear ache
& listens as she reads him *Beautiful Joe*

where sleep & awake underlap
Levi cups a hand to a horse's knee
his hand the shape of an eye

where then & now apex (ISBN/haswas)
the horse in Levi's hand hauls 1911 oak
untofor these eloquent casings I rent

cold gas fireplace vs cable

born listing (ambitious/prone)
I lost the tongue to the cow bell
couldn't find the word 'said'

got the strap (the tongue of the cowhide)
for being the first to carve my name ('lip' & all)
into the soft maple of the new desk

my 3 verb name's point

fill	where these dictates disagree
mane	a rural opera aspires forth
haul	(coxcomb & cigarette paper) . . .

23

leans in this doorway
'the heave shoulder & the wave breast' (Leviticus 10:15)
an offering among offerings
                              unsure & braced

implied lip sing & give

nary sync

I am walking on the thread of my daughter's safety
faltering as I proceed

as she follows me faltering also & laughing
because she cannot see through our floor

& the floors under us to the street
& through spit into grandparent earth

where sadness & fear mesh in a semblance of safety

if she falls into the net her eyes will open
to the dangers of the net

if I close my eyes & dance will I ever find her?

open palm
history's soft spot
hardened
museum skull

dates tread hard littoral water
blot illegibly wave vanish or if
rescued rust fountain mouths off

if Registrar Of Births be deaf

not a word mind not a word
the tools have taken acid

the spirit of the age
grist for the mill

Zeitgrist Ain'tiques

(bicycle own a city
fly own a house)

to the moon right in the kisser

'the *Phils*
beating the *Pits*
6 to 3'

lot

Iroquois
Furrow
Survey
Avenue
Power
Dairy
Archive

concession

cutgrass

Steam
Whistle
Schedule
Chestnut
Coal

stonewall

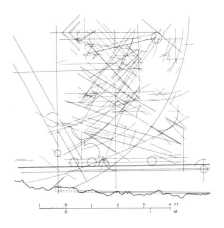

a stone foundation
full of white birches

if the lot had seen the moment coming

on the homestead dump
a partridge bursting

but the moment didn't come up concessions

under a poised foot
3 speckledomed eggs

air planted it on the lightning rod

shadowed by the spokes
of a threshing wheel

then the farm bought in

& lit by the treesun
through a brown Javex bottle
fingerhole

immemorial livestock sped past

the day's reclining
root cellar door flung

squee nameless bills ruffling

nailzedded barnboards
on white grass & cutworms

then the fold shrank
to a lapdog of newsprint

& so where fruit was
done down brambles

a white shirt opens
a carlit gate into a field
appropriated by rabbits

& a sinking loghusk
of mildewed quilts

limey molehairs worried

a grudging boxstove damper

an empty cathandled milk pitcher

                              & rearing
red on flyspecked mounts a brigade
                              now topsoil

still brandishing
dullgreen waterdamaged cutlasses
for noble chins on tuppence

'that dipper hung
a constant in use
by generations at the spring
game shared

floral cups & saucers
never got put to use even
to evoke the old counties
(empty bone murk)

stovepipes thawed
bedrooms with edgings what
drove cast iron orange
in gunracked kitchens

then old pinky rose
(filched wet sweet tin)
drove our triggers off
& slew what we bowed before'

jug quote good cold	too boney
judge dig equation jocund	sliver tractor
quick jog lift little	riding sugar
whiz minimize valve fit vs	wire sapling
health file fat ropes	clickberry
rub passport waxy mainly	smoke tour
vanity intake final yank	suckerpole

people's university unfinished sentence people's university vinegar lightning

afternoons waiting in the gravelscarred beds
of dumptrucks on all fours cocking a knee
barking for sips of I.P.A.

limestone butterballs
menopausal surrogates

midnight little pump in the pantry
cloth to its mouth to catch wellfrogs
honey pail hung from a horn on its upper lip

plastic curtain dahlias
shrivelstinking to Kelvinators

caesarian squinter in torn buggy
careening between tapped maples

right calf sliced pickerelbloodless

snort of bull's magnifyingoggles

aircat meets buckshot safety net

'dear your mother's passed away &
Auntie's going to take you shopping'

'don't like men do you **wack** do you'

sister cramped violent lines to here
to bow to all I ever will of carnage

to call you what I refused to then
this once

Princess

bawl
& rub & rub stumps against stumps

they hit each other over the head
dry cattails snapped on dark gravel

bogseed softening limestones
& them running slapping their heads

rising on the hoof from the swamp
(elevation contours
                    phrenography)

lot confiction survey topograph plowshare

the farm as it was in the head
as it is in their heads
                    as they are now

when open
                    & all the cows bawl
& bleed dehorning day
& rub & rub stumps against stumps

The pibroch opens
*with an **urlar** or ground;*

*continues with a **siabhal***
or a 'moving' of the figuration;

*flows into a **taorluath***
or a sequence of variations;

*and culminates in a **crunluath***
or 'crown'

Epham Nanny

If you ever find an album called *Epham Nanny* – I want it.

I know it exists, because somewhere roundabout 1968 I had a copy of that album, I'm sure, although it is beginning to take on mythic proportions.

The picture on the cover is an archival photo of either the Hatfields or the McCoys. Grey, poor, lanky, long-bearded, grim old men and near boys mesmerized by sulphur, holding very still, holding their civil war long rifles and revolvers very still, on a grey, never-painted stoop.

My album jacket was peppered with holes. A previous owner had shot at the Hatfields or the McCoys with a pellet gun. The vinyl disk must have been luckily out of its slot during the shooting.

How this album wound up in a foreign country, in cottage country, in a rummage sale, in my affinity-palsied hands (and out of them again) is a story I'd like to hear or tell.

The only song I remember is the instrumental 'Red Wing': crude, melodramatic sax. But the general import of the rest of the tunes, as notes explained, was: amateur hillbilly bluegrass enhanced by whoops, grunts, squeals, flubbsters, whistles, honks, yips, barks, mrows, moos and – any vaguely livestockish sound – all made by the musicians as they called around the vocals of the singer.

The notes said that when you really got into the hills you found players who were bored by the empty holes in standard bluegrass music. (Empty holes in bluegrass, that licketysplit, fox-on-the-run, banjo treed picker's challenge?)

So these Hatfields or McCoys just let out rips of caterwaul whenever they heard a hole in the scramble. The result, as I remember it, mythically perhaps, is akin to rural history on fast forward or rewind.

Cacophany from the creaturely world goes into our speaking clearly. We speak from within a stillness that comes of carrying run-to-ground sorrow fervently, as if it were the last live coal of this species. If I carry my sorrow-ember far and long enough it ceases to be my personal sorrow. Then from within its glow can be heard a cast of thousands enlisted from each station of the pecking orders: music not of sorrow but of spontaneous survival-frivolity.

If you find that album, remember, I want it. (Gruntweet) I want to recreate that sound (pergottle). Call it a syntactical folkways endeavour (bunk). Call it applied nonsense (ringong): that syllables and phrases backtracking upon themselves may embellish the music of content.

Applying language jazz to 'amateur' flatpicking ahshucks confessionals: living on Foggy Mountain as we do, we'll use any animal in us to break it down.

yellow canoe

at the end
of an unplowed service road
in a rented cottage on Pidgeon Lake
shore-windowing Boyd's Island
one winter by book
alone he

could not help
hear under ice-roar
his childhood doctor snowmobile
& bloat

or see on the island bison
mothered & cowboyed by grandfather Levi

grazeless dawn mournaments

their sire 'Napoleon' a head
in the local municipal office

or call forth in old groans
against the futtocks of a punt & again
on blackberry-scented cutgrass

the snapped & squeezed milkweed hum
of sunburn first love is

built this yellow canoe
he intended to ship to Greece
& sleep in

take his visiting children out in
sing with gusto & laughter from

>upbraiding myself to audibly curse
>I know what hiding in trees begets

>have slept with a cop but prefer a nurse   . . .

without cures the moving target
Hall is walking through the universe

as bad as it gets inventing worse
makes Death an able opponent I take bets from &
dancing with Zorba am a sack of regrets

cakewalking through the universe
almost always far-flung or never too terse

singing chansons 'til forced to forget
laid low & prettied by skills learned first

backstage in green rooms where Death coerces me
to take a non-speaking walk-on in the universe

at the end
he said 'it's ever now
a non-issue: perfection

there are spoor-melodious imperfections
caulked sound: retsina barrels with pine gum

perfections as bilge-discredited
as the alle*gored* drapery folds of Europe'

(yellowed brush/ feta dipped in Bushmills)

at the end
he said 'Put in my canoe
(unfreighted & never wet)
the following provisions

*my two volume **Lives of the Poets** by Johnson*

my tenor banjo (ivory pegs)   . . .

my 16-gauge
& the toy cannon from Edinburgh Castle
         D'Arcy lost on the train to Aberdeen

full of nectarines my blue & white bowl
& dully pink my tin half-litre carafe

my custodianship of raindrops 350,000,000 years old
         fossildrops around tracks in stone

                (the 3-toed Mother-Of-Us-All
                loping through bog-downpour
                into rockhound/midwife arms)

'It's A Wonderful Life' (uncolourized)

my photo of Simone Weil
         *— the one I wrote 'to **Phil** with love' beneath*

the time Lawrence & I walked under Vancouver
         through the tunnel of muck dug for the coming subway

*my **Bullfinch's Mythology** (Casa Loma gift shop)*

my hoya — toward the day it ever blooms
         velvet stars dripping honey!'

our flight over the Parthenon
         in a NATO 19-seater bucking
         & Brett asleep in my arms

my 37-pound muskie (ambitious/prone)

not just any golf club / guitar — essential it be
         the fretted 2-iron shown to me near —'

(none of this may still exist)   . . .

'my "ultra / left" button
my silver horse-&-saddle pin
my "make poetry useful" button

my beaded string-tie from Manitoulin Island

the marginoclastic **Collected Poems** *of D. H. Lawrence*

the fox I met in the snowfall at the cow-pond

my bodhran
    & my debts nipped with a shrug

my beanbag moonman

Acushla Acushla Acushla ...

& my glasses

but throw my ashes after me
off Little Bob Bridge

suspend my readied canoe
from a blue ceiling
(neither a private collector's nor municipal)

& ripple your hands as you pass under ...'

so ripple your hands as you pass under
his haberdash-catafalque pointed both ways

& read a quote painted where a name might have been
if he hadn't thought names were whitecaps in vaults:

'Sleep! In your boat brought into the living-room
supreme admirer of the ancient sea'

assembly-weeping

grapefruit

my daughter & I dripping at either end of whom's canoe

(*out-take:* pity the underwhelmed)

❂

bulbs

as I lifted the usual cup
to my lips in the pitch room
light enabled me to see
the cockroach in the wine

– can't sleep: light shorting
from loose   in marrow

pound calves with swollen fists
plow drifts k.o. bright

unturned memory rots cold on cold spits

without the cockroach's hiroshimmering
indestructability I'd be
tightened   each with a blown smudge

unscrewed & shaken: my tiny knell

(*out-take:* philament)

one struck by thought
stopped
    facing us &
head to side
quizzical
      unseeing
chased thought

as if gone
    we witness

duende come &
loft its arms in its cloak
so night comes on

– disarming laughter
lopped cry

(*out-take:* bury all ephemera)

to sleep

a thought swung back against
the body a flock of crevices now

(the cliffpin's anchorage joggled)

can't smack into its wherewithal
as it had thought to but wheels

spelling gravity with shadow salvage

(a breath's falling rope-whirr)

(*out-take:* lexicon carny age)

after he cut cheese off his feet
he had me forage bloody dandruff from his scalp
dig a flake & pull it up its hair

dig a flake & pull it up its hair
nails oily & full
                debauch of dark failure

I am full of his defiant failures
& my mother's floor-staring acquiescence
why does dad prune himself mom it's me do you hear?

their deaths bequeath dilapidated pride & vacuity
 – a dustball compost for my credence
who was not born to serve hands-on silently

or vie for attention with other motes of dust
is edge-to-self all you would startle to hear?

(*out-take:* zippered glass yet to be dreamt)

because of what happened to me at 5
I can't sleep beside my son or bathe my daughter
innocently – yet a diaphragm between thoughts & deeds
between lungs & guts

between bellows-winged seraphim

& burros jingling up the mountainside
laden with cases of toilet paper

is – like Joseph the dream-truster
a god of mine – praised be its supple tenacity
as my children leap off the earth
& are lodged in all they do not choose

(*out-take:* in furs they'll swoop & kill each puppet)

❀

each tear has given a muscle
the purple smell of white lilac

so a father can walk to a park
on a cane in pyjamas at dusk

gather grapefruit peels from grass
relive a daughter toddle slurp

each muscle has given a tear
the purple smell of purple lilac

(*out-take:* nostalgia = tooled guilt)

❀

I who am a mess & a failure
at everything words refer to

believe in absolution
by exactitude of usage

my only autonomy in this dilemma

aesthetics come to seed in darkness
skills forced from resolve

retreat into folk hermetics

I who am a flip-book of *sorrys*
begin to discern an algebra of pride

– not in the self
but in what selves may refer to

(*out-take:* myth = my/math)

✾

our weights compact to paths
journewals to inventories

yet florafests – besmirched – our goddess
in whom chemistry worms air

& spring grailworks despite us again up
through knee-wetting fallu*top*ian soil

(*out-take:* gripe water)

✾

wallow-fecund **my**
bean plants lift

fetal-nighted
hang-doggedness

the old tamped first beans split &
borne up on their own bifurcations

bifurcautionlessness
of first leaf-twainings

obligato aqua
(forget **my**)

(*out-take:* church people run funny)

❀

wash the bowls & set them out
wash your hands & set them out

say of thanks for to receive
& wait

by the rhythms of this readiness
shall come sweet potatoes & black-eyed peas

steaming as the spirits who serve them go back
for more sour cream & unsalted butter

from thin blue light come hope's utensils
hope is work do not be ashamed

wash the bowls & set them out
wash your hands & set them out

say of thanks for to receive
& wait

(*out-take:* luck & hope = condiments of grace)

✤

as we peddle through St. James Necropolis
    calling out the names on the stones

her repeating them after me (*Spottiswood*
    Spottiswood makes her giggle / we know a *Hughes*

a *Hughes*) a piper elbowing in the chapel
    is leading warm ashes to scattering-paths

as she is learning to love words
    these bubbles in these levels in this maze

her body side-saddle the cross-bar
    – how ligament-light & unsymbolic

we (though mostly runaway service vehicles
    full of rolled snow-fence careening) can seem

bicycles echoing names half-lost
    – breathshapenly colloidal

these bubbles in these levels in this maze
    essentials pared to *nearly* nothing *nearly*

(*out-take:* epiphany kneaded / rises homesteadable)

✿

alphabetize the obvious

we died by all manners
of closeness here once

yet seen from afar
might be we'll form coteries
seemingly equidistant

where mostly we heard/knew of
each other – corresponded/joined dots

tattoos crowing 90! 91!

kalamatas drydocked between unapologetic teeth!

a constellation might be we'll amount to
some god/dess beast unworshipped/unfeared – the obvious

(death-dots in a hologram appendix to a thesis)

(if heads still wrench back wonder)

cuff these ashes!

(*out-take:* detail = liquid crystal)

✿

healing-song

as if from a skin
suicide disengages itself from the will

ranges along parapets
& stares wistfully out to sea

though my colon's little face gets
shoved into its pocket mirror still

its tongue's blood ancient history
its crooked smile a report just in

(*out-take:* I'mmanent)

convert (Serenity)

'I was hiding inside a dog with the runs and a nose full of porcupine quills. When the dog died, when I climbed out, I was convinced that inside me, back of my navel, a *daemon* slept under an overturned shotglass/hummingbird's nest, and would remain so until I drank again, which would unravel the glass and awaken the *daemon*, who would then grow, fill my form from inside and scream out through my eyes insane for more.

'Gradually I stopped needing the legend of the sanctuary I had become for monstrosities. Instead, I envisioned open, purple morning glories, chakra trumpets hovering ahead of me. I spoke of having tied those glories shut each night for years so any light could not tempt me open.

'Then, just as I seemed to join herds of livestock, just as I gave up my quest for Grail-Notes – out of my head grew the empty hands of the dead: naked they stood in their coffins and raised their arms heavenward. Their arms grew, & hardened, until I had ten points of awkward bone to accountenance for – hat-rack for my head to chauffeur. Beseeching The Above for Grace had hearthedralled the very plates of my skull. I had never felt so noblessedly Animal.

'I had not joined the domesticated herds, but left them to join the spirithood of a Wild.

'Bark is succulent and plentiful on both sides of Death's little stump-fence.'

living ministries

our oak doors the Fire Marshall outlawed
lean dark & indecipherable in the workroom

too majestic to bandsaw &
'let's face it – too *wooden* for safety'

these steel doors we co-operate behind
disguised as wood by a thin veneer of wood
have the optimism of AM radio
                                        – or Jesus Cadets
who extend their living ministries on buses

the original door to my bachelor weighs
more than I do when I hold my daughter

up so she can see the church across the way
  – now home to the Toronto Dance Theatre

planed about 1910 – that door's
tightest whorls were conducting sap
when Percy Shelley & Mary Godwin
did it first against her mother's headstone

my deposed door flaunts an ear-shape
a branch once thrust from & sprouted

I say I hear an oriole's nest hang & sway

hear an oriole orange & black on its two eggs
& its song pirouetting orange & black

                                        – my wooden ear
brings in all this lost gestation the way a disk
monitors gibberish fragments from space: *zilch gist*

I am not all that gungho for the past – imagine
part of Mary Wollstonecraft's chiselled name
imprinted against young Mary's cold bottom awhile   . . .

– see the blood on the flounce
& then try to sing *Barb'ry Allen*
without puking …

but I do go down sometimes to lean – the diagonal man –
my ear against the oak door's ear & hear – let's face it –
nothing
reassuring

at stake I'd insist I hear chansons & coronachs

the Fire Marshall knows his job & I know mine
we prepare for conflagrations in our ways

to invoke Amy Cosh

1   – swimmer at dawn
in the Bobcaygeon Locks

– spry hump & hindsight smile

– snow-yellow pompadoured ne'er-cut hair
abreast carp water

– keeper of the first edition
of Thomas Need's *Six Years In The Bush* (he hated)
or *Extracts From The Journal of a Settler In Upper Canada*
(Tilt, Fleet Street: 1838)

– keeper of the fireplace
in the library/chambers your father built
as an agricultural academy for boys

– unbanded fingers wading through hand-written file cards

– *Bomba, The Jungle Boy* purveyor

since your death
Fred Reynolds (the real estate developer)
has poached cleaned & dressed
'the Hub of the Kawarthas'

& is now lobbying for Boyd's Island
where no buildings were ever raised
where no docks yet waver

where buffalo grazed into early fall
(some brainchild to breed them with cattle
& get 'cattalo')

& then my grandfather would swim them
slowly across Pidgeon Lake
& tempt them into Boyd's big barn for the winter   . . .

until 1915
when 'cattalo steaks were in abundance'
                              is the story

              so when the municipal office is locked
take me through the library's side door again
show me the buffalo head above the entrance

tell me how my grandfather wouldn't own a car
how he cared for this Dakotan bull – 'Old Boney' –

how my people continued
to inbreed slur & burst
in condemned log homesteads
sunk in cow fields
into the late 50s early 60s

invite unto my local shame
farflung hunger

Alexander gives his library's ashes to Borges
within whom's blindness ashes are microfiche

unto my sense of not belonging
invite a ghost of otheritage hope

onto islands of repair
                    hidden in the blood
spirit draw me in my utter denudation
from this accidental home

  – rather a shorelessness myth (Panthalassa)
than this incremental commons auravoir   . . .

– after years of reading
local history
I despair
for the uncollectable past
abudge on flow charts

  – childish of me
I know

2 at the back of the library/chambers
   in the 'Amy Cosh Room' gallery

   prospective Ohioan cottage buyers
   being given the local-colour tour

   moss-green outboard-grey

   purse & squint to appraise
   palette-knifed autumn trees

   gladhanded waves thick & chopping

   while a near-resemblance of you
   seeming to approve – chaperones –

   (gnarled gargantuan memory
   its dander in abeyance)

   but in my recurring dream your hour
   perseveres in its *petit point* collar –

   you are swimming at dawn – are Local History herself
    – are kneeing Fred Reynolds in the balls)

idolater (Schlomo)

'I am too old & no longer believe

a man should get down on all fours
& lick the rim of a woman's chamber pot

& beg to be led on a leash through the streets
naked the way we used to

in Bruno Schulz's drawings
  – our dwarfs' tongues on a pilgrimage to Disdain

but once loving a woman too much
starved scared young
                    & then when she was detained

I cut into wafers & ate her underthings

shoved my finger down my throat
to have them back & eat them again like an ape

in Warsaw skeletons were cutting green chunks
out of bombed horses in the streets at night

draping scraps in their pelvic bowls
they'd run
            & the meat would fall out
on dislodged cobbles

they'd stop
            & as they stooped
            to grab back up their only meat
a puce heel-point might step on a handbone
                                            & laugh

  – so wasn't my depravity
at least the phlegm of a prayer?

or an orchid of gesture?   . . .

I swear I could see directly through her
 – at times she became a grenaded church window
& would let none of us hold her together

oh this one
she was as willfully ill-informed as D.H. Lawrence!

humans once had the heads of birds or cats
absolutely she swore *no question*

& the dead envy us our sleep don't try to deny it

sleep is a luxury!

no rest from facing it all at once forever
that's what death is!

Dr. closes your eyes & they become lidless!

after I ripped out the sunflowers
& smashed their faces against the fence

to my jealousy she bellowed *I loved them all!*
& passed the bottle

her optimism had the rectitude of a martyr's stand-in

but I am too old & no longer believe
she was even an ordinary window with smudges

from my face pressed against a clear ankle
watching for a sign of hope
                              even in her disappearance

 – Disdain smoked & cured on the air

 – I contorting under safehouse pillows   . . .

– no unbroken windows from those years

though San Diego Information
used to have a listing for one with the same name
& twice I left tears in a machine – may it forgive me

some poor woman in San Diego
never answers
               & this drunk accent keeps calling

she was old & my messages came
without warning or mercy
               like the pogroms of our childhood

oh this one
she probably never anymore sets foot in the world

she & her cat Undula switch heads
                  & laugh
as they replay me trying to tame our war

my liver no longer sings opera
my heart has foregone its tail

when quiet sometimes I hear you love

simply changing the pillowcases
& humming our outlawed song'

valuable anger (urson)

don't spare me the details
I worship our threatened complexity
am a docent of senile tributaries

crosshatched deadfall
tumbleweeds of micro-lice
ear wax on a bobby-pin

jazz dirt
the coinage the how-to the memoir mistaken
the solipsism of *Gray's Anatomy*

Alphonse Robinette slips me a cold sausage
then shuffles & claps *Yes Sir! Yes Sir!*

Arnold Beaumont dances alone to jazz on Sunday at Horseshoe Bay
(it says 'Arnold Beaumont' in pink marker on his jean jacket)

details pungent as burdock pottage stirred with a wooden spoon
in museums of bad taste – a flawed flow arbiters can't gussy –

a bicycle leans deep into a curve / a truck
an eye doctor's frames melt (insurance art)

afraid to paint water
for fear of another bipolar distortion

'Tengo miedo de todo el mundo,
del agua fria, de la muerte.'
                    (Neruda)

'these are the / quillized *Nineties*
and I am forty'
          (Lowellesque)

I polish & oil historical hinges
(some ages walls – others doors)   . . .

in hinge-gleam circus-warped am
lost in the rope-lowered crowd – the usual

craning to see the palanquins go by

that buttergirl peeking out demurely
has feet as round as *go*-stones

& will be long remembered
for five lines she composed to her absent husband

while the lives of this crowd I am always lost in
mean less than splats of guano on the sea

in 1822 exquisite Shelley drowns
& Matthew fucking Arnold is born

when William Carlos Williams circumcises Hemingway's son
a midwife of excess comes-to on a battlefield of prose

her hands have been bloodied by the root-strictures of words
her eyes are aprons full of news that will be long-derided

 – though the brevities of both men are already a quaint yellow
Gertrude Stein has given birth to quadruplets!

secundination!

with one kiss Ginsberg absolves Pound
& a poetry that would also like to mention aluminum
can be written after Auschwitz

 … while in cold mud the pristine tracks
of those who intuit the value of anger
& use it as judiciously as saffron …   . . .

porcupine quills are full of air
snip the ends the quills deflate
easier then to pull with pliers the quills
from the flaming pudding of the dog's nose

what began as a game for a hot day
the naked child wearing the dalmation's collar
the dalmation gone off muzzling ragweed
the mother playing at holding the leash for the childog

holding her eyes as the aura comes on &

her hands become her mother's alablister hands
each nail a face a grandmother wore off at home

she cups her faces to her mouth
& the roar that comes out
is silence from a hillside sown with women
all dead in childbirth – bleeding *praying praying*
praying for Purity to lift them
                                        & of course there is none
proven – Faith's snake-oil ...

– I doubt/hope deities hear
our *bleeplessness*
the way dogs hear the silence we blow
& come running –

... chased by the real dog headlong smells veer / yowl

above chapped keepsicks migraine sees
through memory's depressionware
tongues of fire patiently not going out
though the gift can never be drawn down
into whittled chestnut or an afghan or –

inertia has its missionless say-so   . . .

but tongue needs tongue
to impose its missions on
  – to translate the unbeknownst into polyglots
  – to whelm quintessence by assembly-weeping
  – to comfort & cover the child who screams & watches
  – (to stop going to Annie's Bar *etc.?*)

she – they – we can't do any of this
we can't even hold this dog still
enough between the two of us or more

so we get downright livid
at this – this splatter-habitted creature
we think of as family
call by name & yes love

almost as if it were from our own bodies
& hate ourselves for loving so much
of ourselves in it – in us – these quills ...

specially at times like right now – *Jesus!*
Jesus wept!
     [illegible]

while the porcupine just floats away
                  just floats away –

(*out-take:* impurity = empathy & depth)

Snake Pt. Rd.

Iroquois
Furrow
Survey
Avenue
Power
Dairy
Archive

Need St.

---

passéiste

Steam
Whistle
Schedule
Chestnut
Coal

taskmast

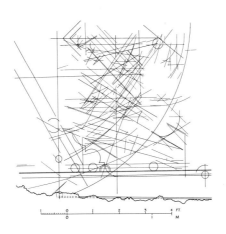

meatbird
      whose head hand
whose beak pen
         whose crest knuckle
whose heart folded lifeline
           adios
(take heart out
      glue to sternum
paint dayglo*medici*
        & let tubes dangle)
              adios

meatbird
      whose song ink
whose flight
      open waving armhigh
          adios

(feet transparent creamfork shadows
thonged to gauntlet)

hear that doing
bird stops
     flits *in absentia*
seen seed

cardinal mating cry

rivet Sunday raindoubt yardsales
to late Saturday conflagrations

while sexual we forget
awhile how rapists inflank us

swangel quieten bells
encircle tongues & lower lips
in netheregions of warm fog

(locked corpuscle door
   permiable blessing

locorpuscledor
   permiablesing

   loper cormia publes clin gedor

locked corpuscle door
   permiable blessing)

then settling remember
& resume stance for cries outside

'singed song'

(to live above beauty)
Genevieve for instance

who plays freelance violin
when she isn't nursing
or reading Jane Bowles at random
into a telephone at a party
while blowdrying her hair

(impromptu performance piece)
she's just come off shift
rushed home showered & rushed here

last night's rehearsal
I screamed at our new bass player

he's too nice right? you just know

there are jackboots & dinky toys
behind that smile

it takes audacious quality to
(Genevieve for instance) &

to free me of anecdote

a woman whose friendship
could not overripen
by more than a drunken kiss
tasting of feta

a woman pivotting cameraward
on the transcontinental

shouting Newlove from memory

waving Bliss Carmen's ring
at burning textbooks

put the cork in the candle
drew Dali whiskers on me

forked me artichokes
fried in lemon juice with garlic
as good as 10 mothers

posed with me with Santa
then sent me to Crete

history's blue oregano
indelible on me thanks to her
faith in my male decency

& anecdote nothing

to live is to fly inside words
not stories or people

the pridespeed catholicity of the edukatydid iamgination

vs

the stumpjumping deadringer selfiant horseshoes post haste heart

*

the moon was a ghostly galleon upon a stormy sea

vs

'pig's arse & cabbage'

we fell is too passive   *headlong dove*
& there were no poems or songs

joylore sniffing its rhythms afresh
our paws on each others' descent   *dove*

for the olive branch of gravity
hooped ripple

& caterwaul on floating docks
pitifully well

*

oh the animals come
to the church in the wildwood

& we come to paper

which offrhymes in a low growl
with *prayer*

killdeer feigned
splintneed then rose
banked & compulsed by otherlove
again & again flopped so

so cold exonoration
if to hatch safe poems alone
& nudge from each a stunt proud
dodo/minion

sigmature

Iroquois
Furrow
Survey
Avenue
Power
Dairy
Archive

in absentia

---

confiction

Steam
Whistle
Schedule
Chestnut
Coal

momace

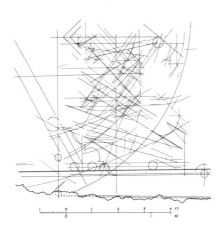

attacked by a chainsaw
while prayerless in hearthedral

scrotum sternum voicebox chin
nosebridge softspot high thought

halved & kicked about shieldfields
'til allsaintless undefinable

*

in an unscrewed upturned cymbal
a jazz great frying peameal on gas

the small white knobs of the sticks
dinging
       char
            turning yellow meat

grease
      leaking outdown the wingnut hole
into flames leaping backupthrough

hones
      glaring 3rdegree rushstroked
saltpork copper
          dinging

meat boy no one sees sees me his mask
meat boy upon whom nothing dries ever

meat boy hold still don't smear posterity
for everyone mesmerized by sulphur

meat boy this memask is your touch proof
coward! passéiste! collusionist! survivor!

meat boy this meatmask wants in

*

imperial
above an africa
of sweetmeats
thought

integrity integered

tweezes
beastial redemption's
vast lean olive
swoop

irony in hoosegow
speak O Toothless One
pagod

the masks in the words

'Land o' Goshen!'   'she percows'

vs   vs

Atlantic Ocean   'sheep or cows'

significant & *voluptuous*
pronuncevasion

& the official accemptance *(vs pawfete typuns)*
of being I is not

mask of 'm' mask of 'g'
mask of 'am'

Serenity comes with an entourage of boistrosities

'we'll use the roofdeck for fencing lessons
this colander if bent will fit a face

the basement's perfect for brewing potato champagne'

no one can hear themselves think above Johnny Horton
they ran through the briars & they ran through the brambles

*

'mesmerized by what you understand
ambitious without product
your models all contemporary

(enter the pen whores: entrepreneurs)

a prize in your voice like a cork

& our souls relying on you'

panned for runes
inside microphones

hung poisoned bait
where clappers swung

boinging harpjaws
put teeth on edge

zilch gist

whatever words meant
has filigreed & transmutated

in the eye corners of new words
nile silt

(what the old words never meant
drops twins)

bapdismal

Iroquois
Furrow
Survey
Avenue
Power
Dairy
Archive

delation

hearth

Steam
Whistle
Schedule
Chestnut
Coal

germina

asleep July tourist heat 1973
4 a.m. your mom from near Arena

over locks (clanging blue) bridges
open window her eyes bookish aflame she

just read **The Luck of Ginger Coffey**
never so radiant as by Moore then

so marry make you & can't read
that germinabook to this day

*

your mother's lifesized selfportrait
of you & she in profile 7th month

her hair long then to small of back
& youmbilic inunder her blue smock

she painted a fridgebox & cut a slit
between feet to make freestanding

her hands on her lower back cupped
your weight stuck wayout blue

that selfportrait in the attic window so
coming home from classes waving **Cathy!**

Andrew! talking to you before episiotomy
forceps & delation made you actual here

waving to an image of your mother if
that cutfridgebox was here now I'd

kiss it as I knew her then kiss its
smockswell 'til my lips were blue

birdless fogdoubt slushclay knolls
crimped treadsmear steppingsaway

mustard bulbs graduantly woolened
cock palm to dankbark & strain

detect 'whitesque' late air's ecolallia
outwait pawbacks to domestic hiss

(each icecube in its bachelorette
each egg in its condominium)

smear love on amnesia's gleaming icons
defile poor memory's untended altars

woven shotglass
old hummingbird nest

snow egg
drip

... love you

implied the *I*
couldn't make it
before death

could not attend
loss later
without religion

became deified
absence implying just
(if *I*'d) guilt

*

(clichés coalesing
architecturally

each radiant joist
an ass-patched syllable

no less a spire
for all its pennydreadfulness
happened once

cliché of 'once')

I can fly at will
(am afraid to do so)

outside all artistry
as I lie down
I swear by my living children
this is true

one shroudleap hugs heaven

but a frog is in the oriole nest
where the trunk of the tree comes up through the floor
& the marriage bed anchors to the high stump (Ygdrasil)

sway nest sway bed
sway cornerstone & peeper

but the egg has on it cold webbed toes

orange turns & dries
the intact speckled shell lightens
the will is such a twig

& 'you will recall my baby toes
have no nails
    mere indentations
from which poke soft claws'

(over the side drops a condom
into an open water lily

on the reservoir tip a moment
a dragonfly)   . . .

the frog hops on the egg
the nest slings the wind
the bed springs chime
tree house & I to rest

swell
imperilous bells
I try

by putting my will to sleep
to fly inward to my unborn children

Iroquois
Furrow
Survey
Avenue
Power
Dairy

littoral **Archive** *vaud*

---

futile given its proximity
to the overly rhetorical
stanchions equivocate between
monument and instrument
ephemerality in the enigma
displaced superimposed
illegible but commemorated

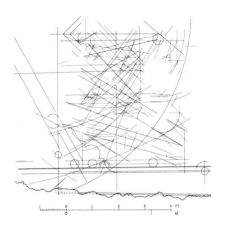

hairy words
have woken me
                disorrified

to money odd
                duty curious
health a racket

                hope a virus
of narrowing apertures

to squalled furbs
                & landescapes
scryved asunder

(vallejo tributaries
                bean runner jesuits
skipping rhymes wafting through
                        desecrated helexi)

retracing to the impass of local birth
push one boot through &
finding a station to lodge against
give a hard shove

inch forward you stalled float

if I don't bite the long dead
I may make here whole

*

Here is a stone flag I sniffed to try to rouse

in my olive grove office
when old

fevered silver pouches of light
ordained scurries

empty slowly twigto of dust

green sceptic dirge – *ragusts*

spit out pits corpse grey
gnawed drip shine

puckerswayed drip shine

downpour on us up Poor
drench all Hope can't

explain by hitting Pain
with its bapdismal pointer

again downpour on us up
pouring Instinct pentward

arcfailingly downpour on us
unseasonably soak Hope's

pointered pain through so
Despair begins leaf letting

singed thong	Iroquois	*inflank*
cutworm	Furrow	*share*
lot	Survey	*concession*
Snake Pt. Rd.	Avenue	*Need St.*
sigmature	Power	*in absentia*
bapdismal	Dairy	*delation*
littoral	Archive	*vaud*

mudyore/ifn

---

gravy	Steam	*swangel*
cutgrass	Whistle	*stonewall*
passéiste	Schedule	*taskmast*
confiction	Chestnut	*momace*
hearth	Coal	*germina*

---

jerkwater

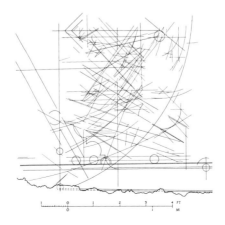

loaf of bread
floating highcurrent
where's Huck?

cannonshot slowing
flight above ripples
where's Huck got to?

visored black spot
waving cane *here's*
Blind Pew I think

almshouse watchchain
espousing decorum *here's*
Micawber I think

as a folkbody beneath sense
rerootstructures origins

begins long floats
up into wet pages
    open hands

wave to selfyeast

pipes play its demise

powerful loving spirits hear us now

help us constantly know we are not
the engineers master-minds or saviours
of this corporeality we are woven into of

keep us receptive to the patient
compulsion of your guidance

powerful loving spirits hear us now

from mortarsinew choruseed
sprout vaudy english

strayhorn hearthedral

exumusicalisthemics

'We live under dark skies and – there are few human beings. Hence, I assume, so few poems.' (Paul Celan, 1960)

'But the gods who are defeated, think that defeat no refutation.' (W.P. Ker, *The Dark Ages*)

Explanatory

Illustration on each list page: the tracing floor above the north porch of Wells Cathedral, France (built 1175-1192), recorded by L.S. Colchester: 'the disappearance of most early constructional drawings is due to their having been traced on the ground or on a floor-slab of plaster made for the purpose. After use such drawings would be obliterated, though the plaster floors used for the purpose actually survive at Wells and York cathedrals, and an important one was in use at Strasbourg until the eighteenth century.' (John Harvey. *The Master Builders*. (McGraw-Hill: New York, 1971)

McCawber, Blind Pew, etc.: *Huckleberry Finn* by Mark Twain, *David Copperfield* by Charles Dickens, *Treasure Island* by Robert Louis Stevenson: because these were early landescapes they figure here, their characters assimilated & bemused along private drawroads of syntax ...

impalpable sustenance: cf. Whitman's 'Crossing Brooklyn Ferry'

this is not me: after Hans Magnus Ensenberger, *The Sinking of the Titanic* (Boston: Houghton Mifflin, 1980)

'Pretty Boy Floyd': the ballad written by Woody Guthrie

Beautiful Joe: The Autobiography of a Dog: Marshall Saunders. (Toronto: M&S, new & revised edition, 1934)

yellow canoe: W.D. Snodgrass's 'These Trees Stand. . .' (1959) needs acknowledgement; & the final quote is by John Berryman, who had Tristan Corbière in mind

Bomba, The Jungle Boy: Roy Rockwood. (New York: McLaughlin Bros., 1926); cattalo: Grace Barker. *Tales Of The Buffalo.* (Fenelon Falls: Dawn Publishing, 1992)

Neruda: from *'El Miedo'*/'Fear' – 'I am afraid of the whole world, / afraid of cold water, afraid of death.' (tr. Alistair Reid); **Lowellesque:** half taken from 'Memories of West Street and Lepke' – 'These are the tranquillized *Fifties* / and I am forty.'

Garlic is as Good as Ten Mothers: a film by Les Blanc; & 'to live is to fly' is a line by Townes Van Zandt

'the moon was a ghostly': first mis-memorized line of poetry, grade 1, Red Rock: Alfred Noyes's 'The Highwayman'; 'pig's arse & cabbage': what Mom always said was for supper

'they ran through the briars & they ran through the brambles': from the song 'The Battle of New Orleans' (Jimmy Driftwood, *aka* James Morris, 1958)

The Luck of Ginger Coffey: Brian Moore. (Boston: Little, Brown, 1960)

'I can fly at will': the italicized lines here allude by sound to lines in section 21 of 'Homage to Mistress Bradstreet' by John Berryman; '& the marriage bed anchors to the high stump (Ygrasil)': 'The mighty ash-tree Ygdrasil was supposed to support the whole universe.' (Bullfinch's Mythology)

'selfyeast': a Gerard Manley Hopkins word, line 12 of [I Wake and Feel the Fell of Dark Not Day]

LAWRENCE MOREY

Originally from Bobcaygeon, Ontario, Phil Hall lives and writes in Toronto, Ontario. He studied Creative Writing at the University of Windsor and often teaches literature for York University. Among his many publications are three other Brick books: *The Unsaid*, *Amanuensis*, and *Why I Haven't Written*.